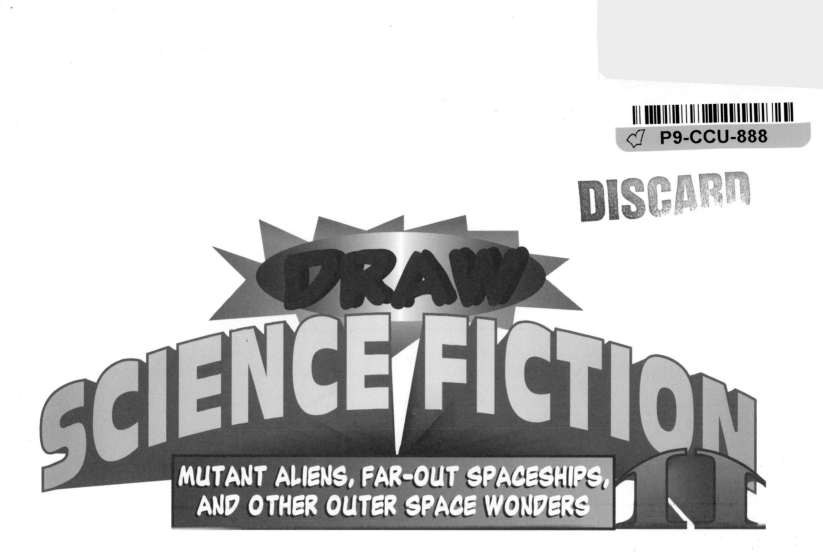

DRAW SCIENCE FICTION II

MUTANT ALIENS, FAR-OUT SPACESHIPS, AND OTHER OUTER SPACE WONDERS

BY THERON SMITH

LOWELL HOUSE JUVENILE

LOS ANGELES

NTC/Contemporary Publishing Group

Published by Lowell House
A division of NTC/Contemporary Publishing Group, Inc.
4255 West Touhy Avenue, Lincolnwood (Chicago), Illinois 60712 U.S.A.

Managing Director and Publisher: Jack Artenstein
Director of Publishing Services: Rena Copperman
Editorial Director: Brenda Pope-Ostrow
Director of Art Production: Bret Perry
Designer and Project Editor: Treesha Runnells Vaux

Lowell House books can be purchased at special discounts
when ordered in bulk for premiums and special sales.
Contact Customer Service at the address above,
or call 1-800-323-4900.

Printed and bound in the United States of America

Library of Congress Catalog Card Number: 00-130076

ISBN: 0-7373-0477-4

VL 10 9 8 7 6 5 4 3 2 1

CONTENTS

In this book, you will learn how to draw fighter pilots, space creatures, galactic vehicles, and other out-of-this-world creations. There are helpful hints throughout to make your drawings come to life. Here are a few tips to get you started.

- Get to know the tools you are using. A pencil will give you a different effect than a pen or a crayon. Try as many different tools as you can to find the ones that work best for you.

- Stay loose! When you are trying to draw a shape, such as a circle, hold the pencil in a comfortable position and draw with your entire arm. Make as many lines as you need to "find" the perfect shape.

- Always pick a light source. If you know where the light is hitting your character, ship, or building, then you will know where to place the shading. This will help make the object you are drawing look three-dimensional.

- It helps to draw center lines down the length of some of your characters. This will show the characters height and helps keep things symmetrical.

- Practice. You are going to make a lot of mistakes, but don't let that get you down. The best way to learn is to look at what you have done wrong and improve on it.

WHAT YOU'LL NEED

Here is a list of some of the tools that you will need. From here, you can decide what else you need to create your drawings. Remember, art tools are not limited to things you find in art stores or your desk drawer. Use anything that you think will make your drawings look better. For example, ash from a fireplace makes a great shading tool!

PAPER
There are many different types of paper that can be used. The most versatile paper is typing paper. From pencil sketches to finished works, it holds up to any eraser and handles ink well. If you want to branch out, try paper with different textures. This will give you a wide range of finished looks in your drawings. However, when it comes right down to it, any paper is good paper—as long as you have lots of it.

PENCILS AND PENS

There are many different types of pencils you can use. Softer pencils are the most versatile. However, the common #2 pencil is still very good for drawings like the ones in this book. You can really go through a lot of pencils in a very short amount of time. A great alternative to the basic pencil is the mechanical pencil. You can get many different types of lead for them and they always stay sharp. They are very useful in drawing ships and buildings because of the consistent line weight they give you.

Another great pencil to try is a light blue colored pencil. You can lay down the groundwork for your drawings (the first couple of steps in this book) in blue and then draw over it with either pencil or pen.

Pens can give you very nice smooth lines and heavy blacks. Felt-tip pens are the best pens to start with. Pens come in various tip widths that will give you different line weights. They are also a good way of adding color to your drawings.

ERASERS AND WHITEOUT

You will find that an eraser on the end of a pencil is never quite enough. You should get several different types of erasers. A kneaded eraser is very handy in removing light lines and smudges. It is also good for removing pencil lines from your finished ink drawing. The other type of eraser you will need is a white plastic eraser. Both can be found in either a small square or a pen form.

Since it is very hard to erase pen lines without tearing through the paper, you will need some liquid whiteout. You can get this in several versions. One is a small jar with a brush. Another is in pen form. The whiteout pen is very easy to use and does not dry out as easily as the brush.

OTHER USEFUL TOOLS

Some other art supplies that you might want to have among your drawing tools are ink and paint. You will need a thicker paper to hold ink or paint and a few brushes of different sizes.

You may also want to find an old toothbrush. You can dip the bristles in paint and hold the toothbrush over your drawing. Run your finger over the bristles to splatter color over large areas to add texture. This technique can be used to splatter a white paint star field for your spaceships to fly through.

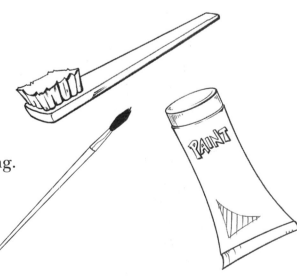

Each drawing has its own look and may require a variety of finishing techniques. The following are just a few of the techniques you may use to bring your creations to life.

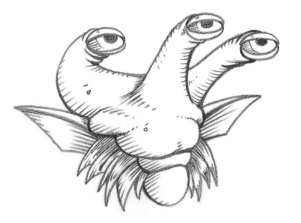

HATCHING

You can create tones and textures by grouping lines together. This is called hatching. For tones or shading, draw straight, consistent lines. For darker tones, make the lines thick and close together. When you want a lighter tone, keep the lines thick and farther apart. You can also use the hatching line to help define the shape of the drawing. Just curve the lines around the rounded body parts to help the drawing look more three-dimensional.

STIPPLE

Stippling is shading and shaping with dots. This method works best with a pen because you can get even black dots with just a touch to the paper. The smaller and farther apart the dots are, the lighter the area will be. On the other hand, the larger and closer the dots, the darker the area becomes. Stipple can give your drawing a smooth gradation from white to black.

BLACK AND WHITE

This style uses only black or white, no grays or halftones. This style is very useful when you are adding mood to your drawings. Anywhere you have a tone that is not white, drop it all the way to black. This is also a very clean way of shading your drawings when you want to make photocopies of your work.

SMOOTH TONE

This style gives drawings a smooth texture. To get this effect, lay the side of your pencil lead flat on the paper and lightly stroke the paper. This will give you a light and even tone. The more pressure you put on the pencil, the darker the tone will become. If you want, use your finger to rub the drawing for an even smoother look. You can go back in with an eraser to get the white tones back.

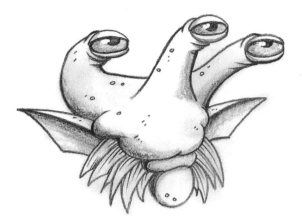

These are just a few of the different ways to finish your drawings. You may want to combine several of these styles to create different textures. The smooth tone works well when drawing plastics, metals, and anything else that needs an even tone. Stippling and hatching work best when you want to show textures in cloth, grit, bumps, and other rough surfaces.

Now that you are equipped with the basics, it's time to start drawing. Let's go!

A dangerous job calls for a clever person. This smuggler has seen his share of close calls when moving merchandise for his employers. He is the best in the galaxy and his price is too high for most. However, in times of great need, people know that they can count on him to fight injustice free of charge.

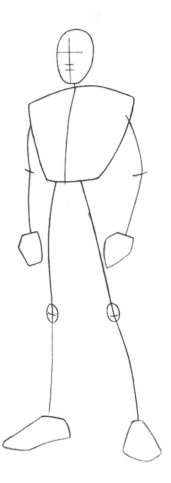

1. Start this drawing with the basic outline of the smuggler's body. First draw an oval for the head. Lightly sketch a line down the center of his head. Use this line to help you place the eyes, nose, and mouth lines. Draw the smuggler's chest, leaving a small space under the head for his neck. Draw a line down the chest. Now draw guidelines for the arms and legs, with lines halfway down for the elbows and knees. The knees can be defined with small circles that will be erased later. Sketch shapes for his hands and feet.

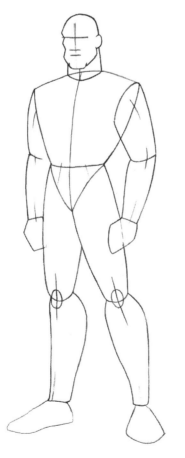

2. Begin to detail your smuggler's head by adding a brow line, cheekbone, ear, jaw, and chin. The top of his ear should line up with his eye line, while the bottom should line up with his nose line. Using the guidelines, add the neck, arms, and legs. Lightly sketch the pelvic area in a *V* shape to better understand the placement of the legs and, later, clothing.

3. Now add some facial features and his eye patch. Start filling in the clothing by drawing a collar around the neck. Then add sleeves, with thick cuffs above his hands. At the elbow of the right arm, add a couple of lines to indicate a fold in the sleeve. On the left arm, add a band above the elbow and one just below. Draw his belt using the waist guide-line. Add the bottom part of his tunic using a line below the belt and the *V* of the pelvic area. Place some folds at his knees and ankles. Give the boots thick soles. Erase any unnecessary lines.

4. Continue modeling the clothing by adding more detail to his tunic, pants, and boots. Draw a holster and blaster on his right leg. Add utility compartments to his belt. On the smuggler's left arm, start building his mechanical enhancements by connecting the two bands to each other in front and at the elbow.

5. Shade his eye patch. Complete the left arm. Detail the elbow joints and join the elbow area to the cuff at the wrist. Finish his belt by hanging some equipment from it and adding detail to his belt buckle. Give his boots more shape and add pouches to the sides.

6. To get your smuggler on his way before the Supreme Command can catch him, he needs a few more touch-ups. Imagine the light source over his left shoulder and shade his body as shown. Darken the details of his boots. Make the mechanical parts of his left arm look metallic. Finally, add a few specks to the cloth of his pants and tunic.

In Makhonea City, an elite group of police has been selected to become Guardians. They have years of special training in all forms of combat to prepare them for any situation. The Guardians wear heavy armor, and they carry stun rifles that can subdue a criminal more than 100 yards away. The city has been a safer place to live since the Guardians began patrolling the streets.

1. Begin this big guy by sketching a large torso area with wide shoulders. Set an oval shape on top of the shoulders. Draw a center line from the middle of the oval to the bottom of the torso. Add guidelines for his legs and arms with lines at the knees and elbows. Sketch large shapes for the hands and feet.

2. Draw a line down his head. Add guidelines for his eyes, nose, and mouth. Give his face more structure by adding a jawline on his left side. Fill in the basic shapes for his neck, arms and legs. Add a thumb to his left hand and shape the right hand.

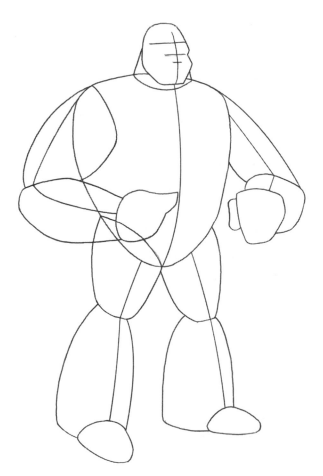

11

3. Add the brow ridge and nose shape. Draw a small line for his bottom lip. Make a small circle at the point where the top of the neck meets the head. Define the shape of his face on his right side. Sketch large triangles over his shoulders. Add a waistline just above the top of his legs. Indicate fingers on his left hand. Erase any unnecessary lines.

4. Shape the brow ridge and add eyes underneath it. Put nostrils on his nose and give your guardian a big frown. Shape his bottom lip. Add a collar in the armor around his neck. Draw gloves and elbow guards. Give him knee guards and add the base of his armor behind his feet. Turn the single line around the waist into a connection ring for the upper and lower parts of the torso armor. Begin shaping his stun rifle.

5. Further detail his face and armor. Give your guardian a big number seven on his chest. Complete the stun rifle with a handle in his left hand and one under his right arm. Erase any unneccesary lines.

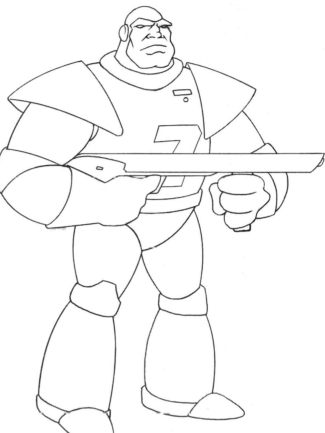

6. To make your guardian complete, add darker tones to the heavier parts of his armor. Give the suit a smooth finish. Shade the face, but leave the eyes a glowing white. Your guardian looks tough and ready for action!

Fighter pilots have the most advanced flight suits. Some of the features are sun-blocking goggles, an automatic pressure adjuster, a micro oxygen tank, and a portable computer. The suit itself may be impressive, but it is nothing compared to the incredible skills that the fighter pilots have mastered.

1. First, draw the torso area. Since the pilot wears a heavy mask, his head shape is basically a cylinder with a rounded top. Add guidelines for his arms and legs with lines at his elbows and knees. Sketch shapes for his hands and feet.

2. Add a pelvic area. Draw a line down the center of his torso and extend it below the waist. Fill in the shapes for his arms and legs. Notice that most of the left arm will be hidden behind the body. Sketch the pilot's goggles, and draw a light circle to indicate the breathing hose underneath. Draw a rectangular box with a circle in the middle for the air hose.

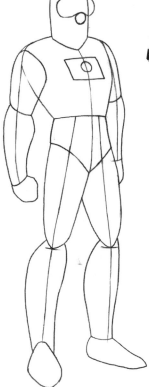

3. Detail the goggles and add an earpiece along the side with a small circle in the middle. Add the hose running from the nose to the box on the chest. Give the box a 3-D effect. Draw a collar around the pilot's neck and cuffs on his sleeves. Add shoulder pads, as well as flexible disks to his elbows. Start giving the pants some shape with folds at the knees. Add the pilot's boots just below his knees. Erase any unnecessary lines.

4. Add an antenna on his ear, a strap joining the goggles to the earpiece, and the lower part of the faceplate. Draw straps over the shoulders and around the waist. They all come together at the box on the chest. Under the box, add a cylinder with a circle at each end. Give the pilot two belts, one hanging slightly lower than the other. Sketch a line around his right leg for his holster. Add folds to his sleeves and shape his right glove. Draw lines for the metal shields over the foot of each boot.

5. Before shading the pilot, add a few more details like his blaster and holster. Add segmented lines on his breathing hose and on his boots. Draw some gauges and buttons on the box on his chest. Add a hose to the cylinder under the box. Detail the belts, buckles, and cuffs of his sleeves. Erase any unnecessary lines. Add some shading and tone and your fighter pilot is ready for his next flight.

These soldiers' suits have a recycled air system and enough food and water to last three days. With the help of the small rocket pack on their backs, deep space soldiers can fly almost as fast as small spaceships.

1. Begin by drawing the torso shape of the soldier. Attach a thick cylinder to the top of the torso for his helmet. Add the center line of his torso, closer to the soldier's right side. At the bottom of the center line, sketch in a line with two small circles at both ends. This will be the hip area. From here, add guidelines for the legs with lines at the knees. Add shapes for his feet. Draw guidelines for his arms with lines at the elbows, then give him shapes for his hands.

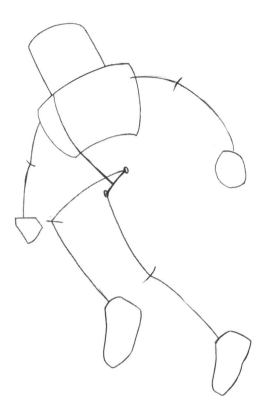

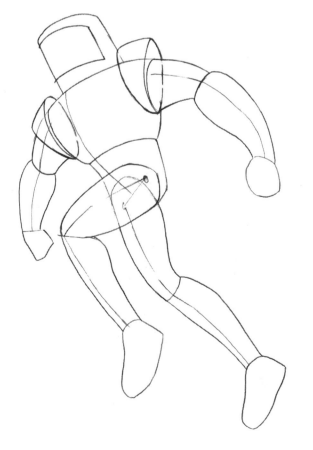

2. Add a curved, rectangular shape on his helmet for his glass visor. Sketch in the shapes for his shoulders. Outline his arms and legs, building the legs around the small circles at his hips. Draw the pelvic area, connecting his legs to his body.

3. Add a defining line inside the front of his visor. Sketch a large box on the back of the soldier. This will be his jet pack. It helps to draw the entire shape of the box even though you will not see most of it. Add gloves and fingers to the hand shapes. Draw bands below his elbows and triangular shapes on his knees. In his left hand, sketch an oval shape with a guideline down the middle. Add the tops of his boots and the soles at the bottom. Erase any unnecessary lines.

4. Complete the jet pack by first adding a hose from the top of the pack to the back of the helmet. Now add the jet engine to the lower part of the pack. Draw a couple of lines in the pelvic area to indicate folds in the soldier's suit. Add a rectangular shape at the back of each boot. Sketch the blaster in his left hand with a series of boxes and a circle at the end. Leave a little of the line sticking out from the circle. Erase any unnecessary lines.

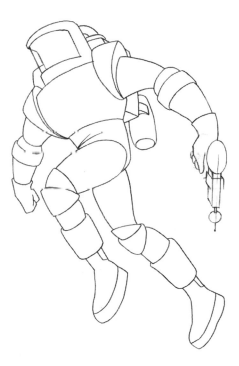

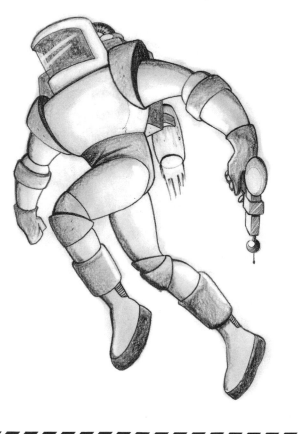

5. Draw blast lines coming out of the jet. Finish your soldier with some shading. When you are shading, be sure to make the light source come from the jet blast. The darkest areas will be on the outside edge of the soldier. Finally, erase some lines to create streaks on his glass visor.

Worker cyborgs have been fitted with neutron-piston joints to allow for lifting the heaviest equipment. Their skin is a high-density carbon-based metal. They also have molecular computer processors attached to their brains to help them solve complex equations.

1. Begin with an almost triangular torso shape. Add an oval head to one side of the torso. Sketch guidelines for the arms and legs, adding circles at the elbows and lines at the knees. Draw the hand and feet shapes.

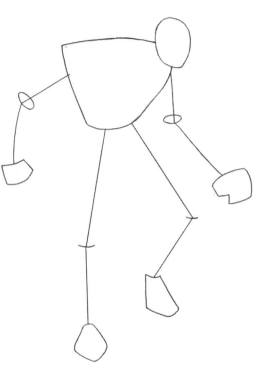

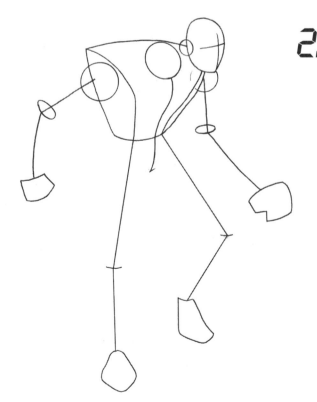

2. Lightly sketch guidelines on the face. Draw a small circle on the side of the head. In the middle of the shoulder area, draw a larger circle. This will connect the neck to the shoulder area of the torso. From this circle, add the center line through the torso, extending it below the waist. Add guidelines for the arms with an oval at each elbow. At the point where the arms meet the torso, add a circle. Draw guidelines for the legs, starting at the topmost point of each side of the torso. These guidelines will define the shape of the chest and torso as well as the legs. Add lines for the knees and draw shapes for the feet and hands.

3. Add a curving shape that connects the neck circle on the torso to the top of the head. This is where the wiring will be. Above each of the shoulder circles, add a triangle that connects to the chest guidelines. Define the forearm shapes for each arm. Add a double *V* shape below the waistline for the pelvic area.

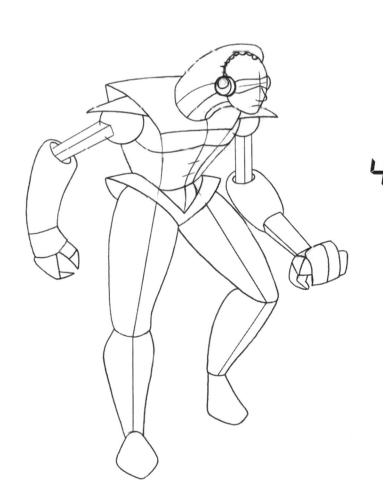

4. Add the nose, mouth, and goggles. Indicate the wiring on the head with a series of tiny semicircles. Define the shape of the earpiece. Add some more lines to the neck area. Just below the neck, draw a horizontal line between the chest guidelines to create the shoulder plate. Under this, add the chest between the two shoulder circles. Sketch small lines for the abdomen plates. Shape the upper arms into long boxes that fit inside the elbows. Add fingers to the hands. Fill in the shapes of the legs and the pelvic area. Erase any unnecessary lines.

5. Add multiple wires to the top of the head and one coming from the earpiece. Detail the abdomen plates and add wires to the sides of the torso. Add a large cylinder to the top of the cyborg's right leg and a hint of one on the left. Draw a cylinder through each knee. Just above the ankles, add small shapes that wiring will fit into. Finish shaping the structure of each forearm and the hands. Erase any unnecessary lines.

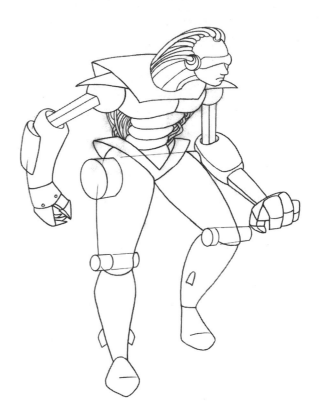

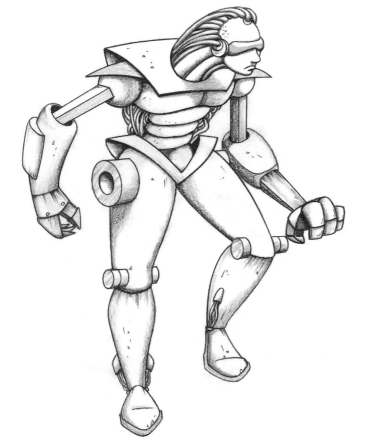

6. To complete your worker cyborg, create a hole in the large hip cylinder. Draw some of the exposed wiring at the ankles, connecting to the feet. Also add some hair stubble in front of the head wires. Further define the facial features and goggles. Add tone and shading to your cyborg to make it look metallic and angular.

Quanis City was built on a large asteroid that moved into orbit high above the planet Vospbor'ne's surface. From here, travel to other planets is much easier, since the long-range spaceships no longer have to leave Vospbor'ne's atmosphere.

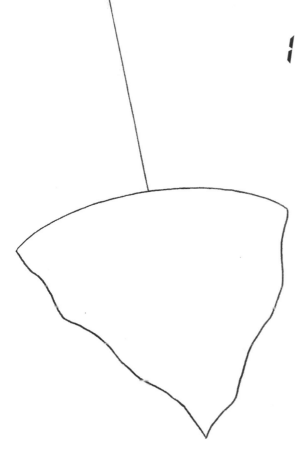

1. To build an orbital station, you must first make a cone-shaped asteroid. Keep the sides of the cone very loose and uneven, while the top should be a smooth curve. In the center, draw a line up from the top. This will be a useful guide for your city.

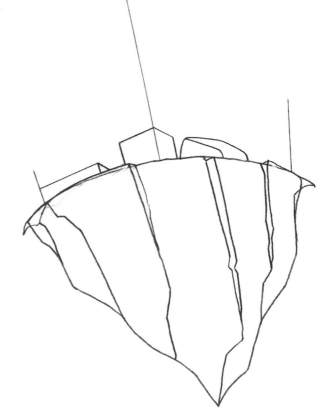

2. Add some jagged lines to create a rocky surface, as well as two more straight lines at the top. Extend the edges of the top of the asteroid a little so they hang over the sides. Begin to draw the buildings that make up the station. Create them as box shapes. Start on the left with a flat box. In the center, add a taller box, and next to it draw a box that is lower on one side with rounded edges.

3. Behind the first three boxes, start adding more boxes that are taller and have various shapes. The building that is third in from the left should be drawn as a tall cylinder instead of a box.

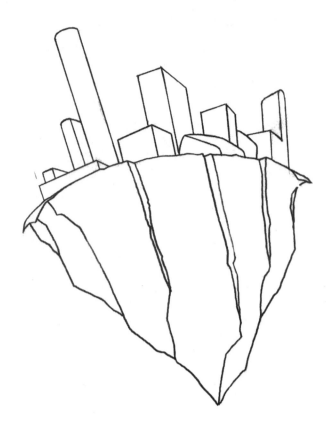

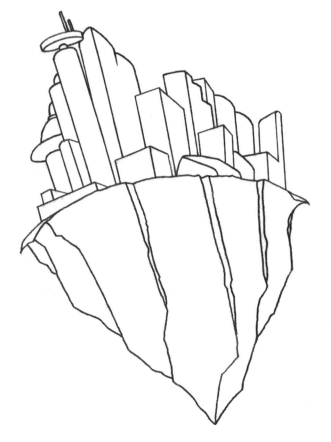

4. Add another row of boxes and some more cylinders with rounded tops. On top of the tall cylinder in the second row, add a disk shape with two exhaust pipes on top. On the left side of the city, create the rounded shapes as shown. Remember, since these buildings are in space, they can be any shape you want them to be and gravity won't pull them apart.

5. Draw another tall building in the background of your city. Add a transportation tube curving from the far right building to a building in the middle. Put an external elevator shaft in front of the building with the disk on top. Now that the outline of your station is complete, add a planet and a moon to your drawing.

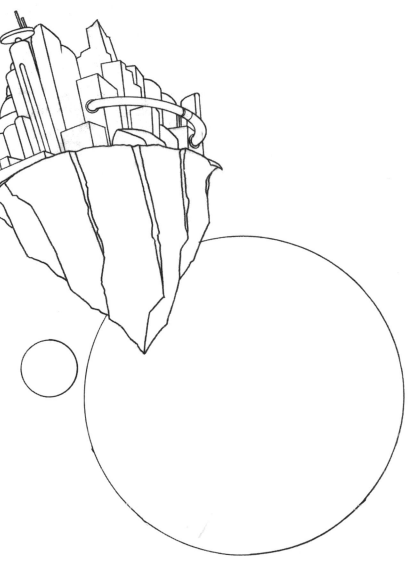

6. Detail the buildings with tiny windows. Give the planet swirling clouds in its atmosphere. Add large dark circles on the moon for craters. Further shade the buildings, the asteroid, the moon, and the planet using this system's Sun-like star as your light source. Finally, add some stars to complete your orbital station.

These air cycles are mostly used on planets where solid ground is scarce. Conventional forms of transportation, using wheels, would sink in the swampy ground. Air cycles are lifted off the ground by an antigravity field and maneuvered with front steering bars.

1. Start your cycle with a pear shape. Add a guideline down the center.

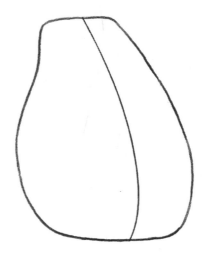

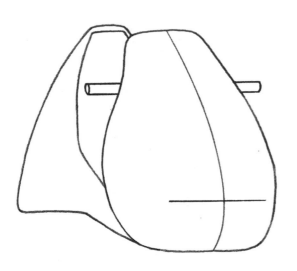

2. Intersect the center line with a smaller line. Draw handle bars a third of the way down from the top. Now add the back of the cycle.

3. Just above the handle bars, add a curved line for the windshield. Down at the intersecting line, add the opening for the front steering bars. Draw a circle on each side of the center line and inside the opening. Near the back and at the bottom of the cycle, draw a footrest. Just behind the footrest, sketch the rear stabilizer bar, which goes straight through the body of the cycle. Erase any unneeded lines.

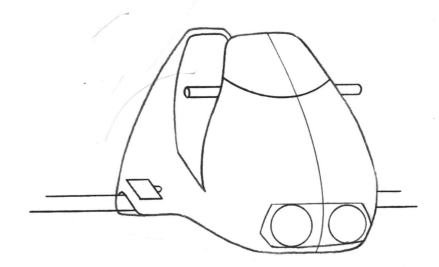

4. Add a stabilizer to each end of the bar. Draw lines coming out from the circles on the front of the cycle for the front steering bars. At the end of these, add the front antigravity unit. Create an edge around the windshield to make it look like it is sitting in the molding of the cycle. Erase any unnecessary lines.

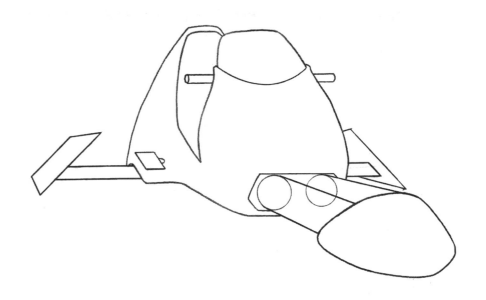

5. Add backrest bars and a seat to the interior of the cycle. Give the rear stabilizers some thickness by adding an extra line. Under the back section of the cycle, add the rear antigravity unit.

6. Finish your air cycle with a couple of brake handles under the handlebars. Pick a light source, and shade to give the cycle a smooth metal finish. Shade the windshield dark, then use your eraser to add white highlights.

These large beasts are covered in layers of thick hair to block out the harsh sun and to keep their bodies warm at night. They also have a long trunk that they use to dig deep into holes or under rocks to find food. Their eyes have an extra, clear eyelid that keeps sand out during desert storms.

1. Begin this massive creature by drawing a large circular shape. Add another, smaller circle to one side. This smaller circle will be the head.

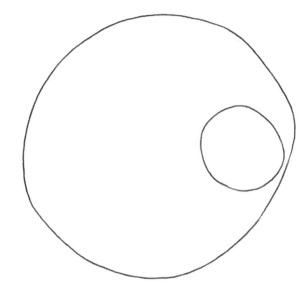

2. Draw a long trunk hanging down from the head. Next, sketch the basic shape of the front and back legs. At the end of each leg, draw roundish shapes for the feet.

3. Start adding some hair lines around the body and head. Break up the feet shapes to show where the toes will be. Complete the shape of the feet by connecting the toe areas to the backs of the legs. Give your beast ears and eyes. At the bottom of the trunk, draw a small peanut shape. Your beast will need this to grip food and put it into its mouth.

4. Now give your beast's heavy-looking hair more detail. Draw drooping lines under each eye. Round out the toes on the feet.

5. Finish your beast by adding more hair lines around the body. Find the light source and shade accordingly. Draw some texture on the feet and trunk. The trunk now looks like it has heavy, scaly skin. Darken the eyes and add a small highlight to make them look wet.

When the people of Earth began colonizing other planets, Mars was their first "home away from home." Entire cities were built inside massive structures to control atmospheric conditions that could support human life. Above the main part of the complex is a skyscraper that houses the citizens of the colony.

1. For this drawing, you need to use a ruler and perspective (see page 63). Start by drawing the horizon line. On this line, you need to pick a point off to your right. Mark it with a small *X*. Now draw a long rectangle rising up from the horizon line.

2. Next, create a large box that is wider at the bottom than the top. On the right, the top side of the box is found using a visual line from the *X* on the horizon. The front top of the box is parallel to the horizon line.

3. Erase the part of the rectangle that is inside the box you just made. Draw another line straight down the rectangle. At the top left of this area, draw a curved line connecting the two lines. Now draw three diagonal lines across the rectangle using the *X* on the horizon as a guide. Add a shorter cylinder to the left of the tall structure.

4. Draw a curved line on the right side, between the second and third lines of the taller structure. Erase the unnecessary lines at the top and side as shown.

5. Draw another curved line at the front of the tall structure. Add another long cylinder to the backside of the tall structure. Connect this cylinder to the top of the tall structure with a curved line at the back. Draw some long, thin tubes at the top of the tall structure and the other cylinders. On the front of the lower structure, add a box that is a smaller shape than the front plane. Then add a line straight down from one corner to the horizon line. On the right side of the box, duplicate the shape, only smaller. Use the point on the horizon to help with the placement of the top and bottom lines.

6. Add some windows to the tall structure. Use the point on the horizon to draw these accurately. Add windows to the front of the lower area by making three long, thin rectangles. Under these, draw part of another rectangle with several vertical lines. Erase any unnecessary lines.

7. Finally, add some shading to your building. Keep in mind that some parts are flat and some are rounded. The shape on the right side of the lower structure will be a large window. Make a few dark streaks with your pencil and some lighter streaks. Go back in with an eraser to make it look like glass. Add some clouds and mountains in the background. Turn your horizon line into the ground by making it look jagged and rough.

The asteroid miners' suits have to protect them as well as help in their work. Inside each suit is a climate-controlled environment with recycled air. The suits are also equipped with powerful titanium drills and hydraulic arms. Each foot has a gravity generator that keeps the miners attached to the asteroid.

1. Draw the torso of the miner, making it larger at the shoulders and smaller at the waist. Set the helmet shape into the shoulders. Add a center line through the torso. Sketch guidelines for the arms and legs. Draw lines at the knees and elbows. Add shapes for the feet.

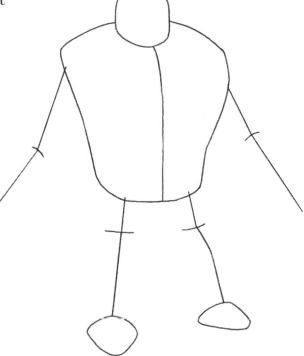

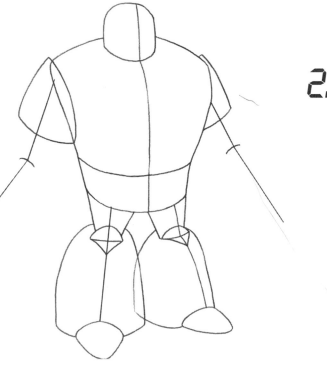

2. Draw the center line in the head. Add a line around the waist in an upward curve. Draw the shoulder guards over most of the upper parts of the arms. The knee area is formed with two basic shapes, a half-circle on the top and a triangle on the bottom. Fill in the shapes for the upper legs. Build the lower legs with large bell shapes.

3. Define the front of the helmet with another line running from the top to the bottom. Next, add a line around the lower part of the helmet. Draw a line out from the miner's left shoulder and add a circle to the end of it. Begin drawing the miner's right forearm with a large cone. Sketch a half-circle at the top of the cone. On the miner's left arm, make an elongated oval for the forearm. Fill in the shapes for both of the upper arms. Draw a square shape at the waist, halfway down the upper legs. Detail the waist area on either side of the square shape. Erase any unnecessary lines.

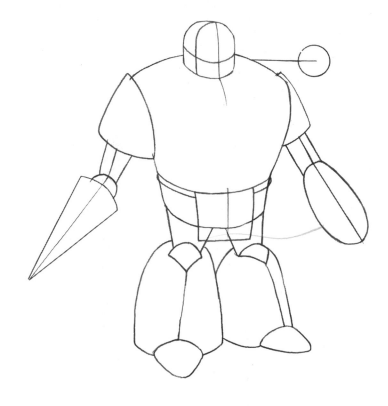

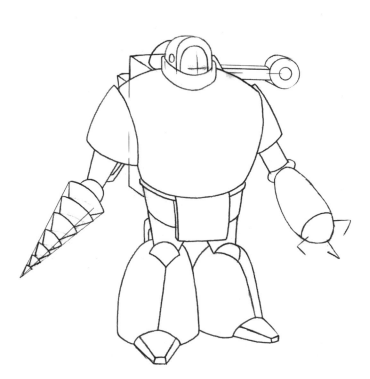

4. Add a large box (backpack) to the miner's back with another smaller box behind it. At the top of the large box, begin the air hose that connects the box to the helmet. Add more detail to the helmet. Put guidelines on the head for eye and nose placement. Fill in the shape of the laser tube on the miner's left shoulder. Break the miner's right-hand cone into smaller segments and add a hydraulic lifter to the upper part of this arm. Add the elbow joint to the left arm, a curved line on the end of the oval, and three lines for the pronged, clawlike hand. Give the square shape at the waist some depth. Add a hydraulic lifter to the miner's right leg and detail the area at the feet. Erase any unnecessary lines.

5. Complete the face inside the helmet. Add detail to the backpack and hose. Draw some tubes on the arms and legs. Also add a large tube to the torso that connects to the backpack just below the waist. Finish shaping the miner's right-hand drill by cutting into the segments with smaller triangles. Instead of fingers, the miner's left hand has three gripping clamps. These are made with two flat rectangles that are connected like a hinge.

6. Finish your asteroid miner by adding shading to the armor. Make it appear dirty by adding specks of dirt. Imagine the light source above and slightly to the left of the miner, then shade accordingly.

SPACE WHALE

Space whales live in a distant part of our galaxy, and they travel between planets without needing to breathe air. Similar to the eating habits of whales on Earth, the space whale moves with its mouth open to take in small particles of rock and black matter.

1. The whale is built from one basic horizontal, oblong shape. It is thicker at one end and tapers off to a rounded point at the tail. Add guidelines for the tail and body fins.

2. Fill in the shapes of the fins. Sketch both sides of the mouth. The side closest to you is a stretched-out *C*. The far side is almost the same but not as stretched out. Now draw a circle behind the mouth and one in front of the body fin. Connect these with a guideline for the eye stem. Extend this line on the other side of the body past the mouth. Add a circle to the guideline.

3. Sketch a rough line on top of the body. This will be a rocky ridge, so the rougher the better. Draw the same type of line around the mouth as rocky lips. Fill in the shapes of the eyes and eye stems. Add a lid over each eye. Make three lines on the body behind the fin. Now draw a series of hourglass shapes inside the mouth for the mouth ridges.

4. Add more detail to the ridge on top of the body and around the mouth. Draw large and small shapes to represent rock plates along the whale's back. Turn any smooth line into a rough line. This will help give the whale a rocky feel. Break the hourglass shapes into smaller pieces and connect them to the top and bottom of the mouth.

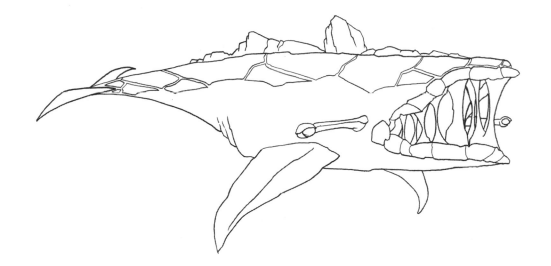

5. Complete your space whale by shading and adding tone. To enhance the rocky feel of the whale's body, add small specks and jagged lines. In addition, use the side of your pencil to make long, straight streaks.

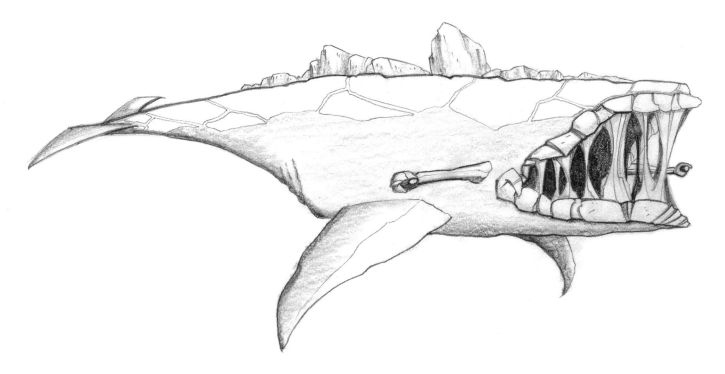

These creatures live on a planet that is very near their sun. Most of their planet's surface is covered in molten rock. To survive here, the lava dwellers' skin is made of a very strong rocklike metal that can withstand extremely hot temperatures.

1. Start this bulky creature with a large triangular chest area. The broad shoulders taper down to a smaller waist. Set a wide oval below the shoulder line for the head. Add a center line down the chest. Draw guidelines for the arms and legs with lines for the elbows and knees. Add shapes for hands and feet.

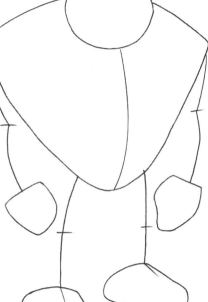

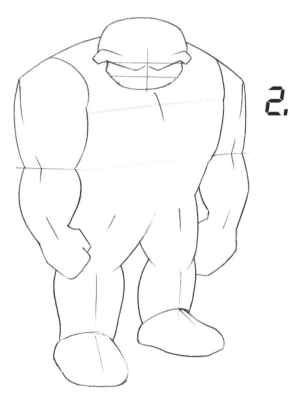

2. Add guidelines for the facial and chest features. Draw brow ridges, then shape the lower part of the head under the ridges. Fill in the shapes of the arms and legs. Add a thumb to the creature's right hand. Be sure to hide most of its left hand behind the large left leg. Erase any unnecessary lines.

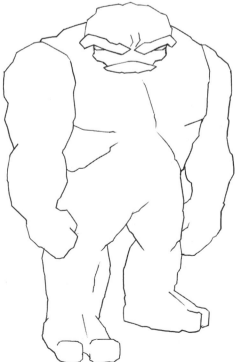

3. Give your lava dweller a rough, rocky outline. Define the brow ridges and place the eyes underneath them. Build the cheekbones, then define the mouth and jaw. Add some detail to the chest area. Create two toes at the end of each foot. Remember to make all the shapes rocklike by avoiding round, smooth shapes. Erase any unnecessary lines.

4. Complete the waist and upper part of the creature's right leg. Continue to define the rocky form by adding more jagged lines, particularly to the head.

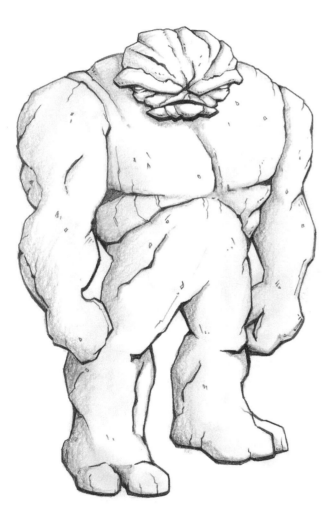

5. When finishing your lava dweller, try using lines with different weights. Add texture to the rocky surface by drawing cracks and chips all over the body and head. Define the cracks and the outline of the body and head with darker shading.

Drawing Tip: While rendering the texture of this creature, it is very helpful to find a rock and look at its surface. In this drawing and any other drawing you do, it is always best if you have some real objects to use as reference. This will make even the most otherworldly creatures look believable.

This galactic cruiser is nearly a mile long. It is a traveling city equipped with a space-fold drive, which enables it to get to any planet in the galaxy in a matter of hours. It is the greatest achievement in space exploration.

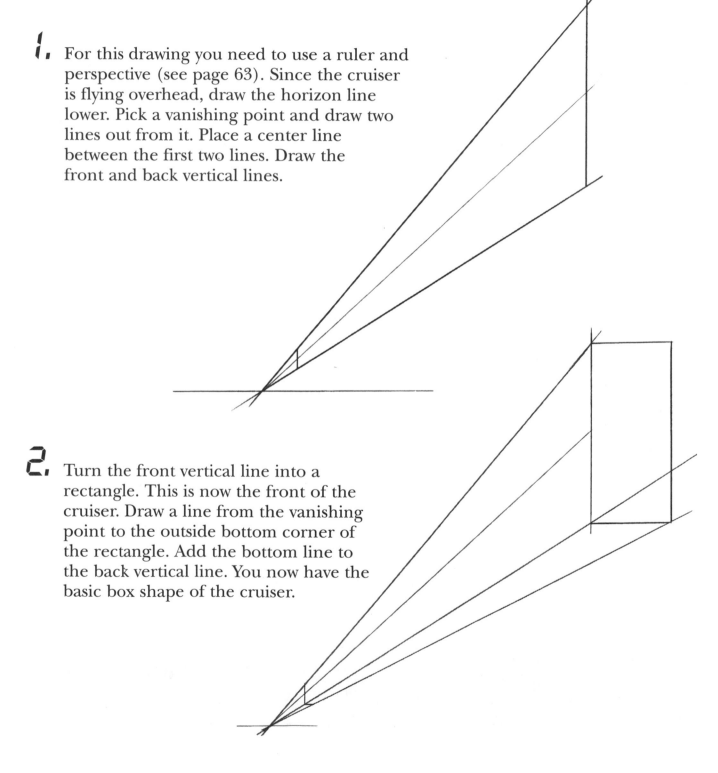

1. For this drawing you need to use a ruler and perspective (see page 63). Since the cruiser is flying overhead, draw the horizon line lower. Pick a vanishing point and draw two lines out from it. Place a center line between the first two lines. Draw the front and back vertical lines.

2. Turn the front vertical line into a rectangle. This is now the front of the cruiser. Draw a line from the vanishing point to the outside bottom corner of the rectangle. Add the bottom line to the back vertical line. You now have the basic box shape of the cruiser.

3. Now make the shape of the cruiser into two large boxes connected with another longer box. The back box is much smaller because it is in the distance. Draw a line through the center of the front box. Erase any unnecessary lines.

4. Break the long connector box into smaller segments. Remember to keep all lines on each side parallel to each other. Erase any unnecessary lines.

Drawing Tip: You need to use a ruler or another straight edge for this perspective drawing. After you try this version, you can go back and try different horizon lines in your drawing and the cruiser will remain the same shape but in different positions.

5. Use vertical and horizontal lines to make a wedge in the top half of the front box. Erase the top and bottom lines in the smallest segments of the long connector box. Turn the remaining segments into boxes. Make the third connector box the largest of that group.

6. Add a flat box underneath the front section. In the section behind the third, larger connector box, add two rectangular solar energy panels with lines. Attach a tiny cylinder to the back section. Draw three guidelines out from the bottom and sides of the back section and add a circle to each line. These will be the engines. Erase the outside vertical lines in the front box wedge.

7. Turn the engine circles into cylinders. Connect them to the back section with rectangles. All of these are created using the same vanishing point on the horizon line. Complete the arms of the solar energy panels. Now join all of the connector boxes with even smaller boxes. Add another box to the side of the large center section. On this new box, add a small piece of a disk. On top of this large section, add two boxes with exhaust tubes. Draw a communications dish on top of the front section and a dual laser cannon to the flat box underneath that section.

8. Finish your galactic cruiser by adding detail to the surface. Use small rectangular shapes and lines to add many small metal plates. The more detail you add, the larger the cruiser will look. Draw a grid on each of the solar panels. Shade your cruiser as shown. Create the background of stars and planets. Since this is deep space, there will be very little light.

Since the galactic cruisers are too big to land on a planet, the planetary shuttle is used to transport people and supplies. Its ion propulsion drive is used until the shuttle enters a planet's atmosphere, then the more standard fuel-burning engine kicks in. The shuttle can carry 10 people and over 20 metric tons of cargo.

1. Start the shuttle with a box that is curved at the back end and pointed in the center at the front.

2. Add a line that runs from the bottom of the curve to the center point at the front. Continue the line on the front of the box. Draw a triangular-shaped box at the front of the shuttle. The base of the triangular box attaches to the bottom of the main part of the shuttle.

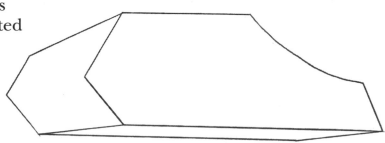

3. Draw the dome in the curve at the back of the shuttle. Add rectangular engine stabilizers to the near and far sides of the shuttle.

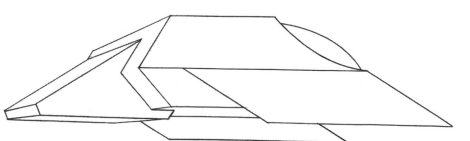

4. Give the stabilizers some thickness and add cylinders at the bottom edges. Draw the windshield on the front of the shuttle. Sketch a curved blaster base on the top left of the shuttle.

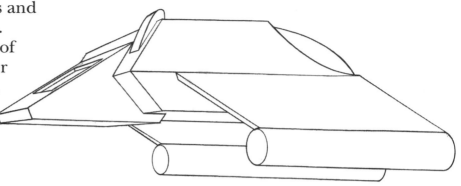

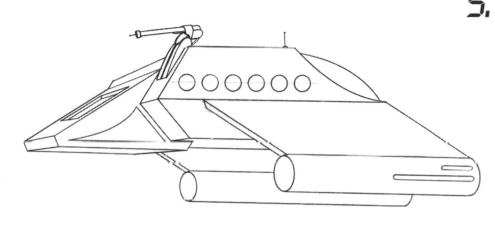

5. Create a blaster on top of the blaster base. Add a track line down the center of the base. Draw a row of windows along the side of the shuttle. Place one long tube and another shorter tube on the side of the near engine cylinder. Complete the front side of the shuttle with a triangular shape that is curved on one side. Draw a small communications antenna on top of the shuttle.

6. Complete your shuttle with light and dark shading. Add some symbols along its side. Use your eraser to create highlights on the dome and windows.

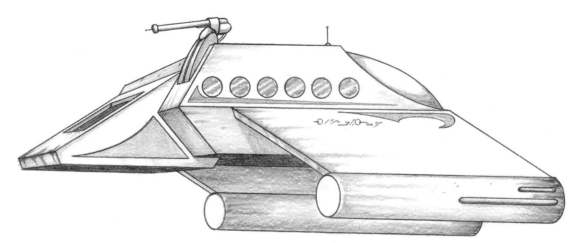

These bird-people have built their homes and cities in the massive trees that cover most of their planet. They have designed a very strong plastic covering to wear over their wings that helps them fly faster and higher.

1. Begin the bird-man with a lemon shape for its head. Make the bottom more pointed than the top. Draw the torso area. Sketch a guideline for each of the wings.

2. Add the center line of the head and a line for the eye placement. Draw the upper lines of the wings using the guidelines. Add guidelines for the arms and legs with small lines at the elbows and knees. Sketch shapes for the hands and feet.

3. Draw long sweeping lines for the bottom edge of the wings. Add the pelvic area below the waist and fill in the shape of the legs. Draw pointed toes on the feet. Fill in the shape of the arms, then add thumbs and fingers on each hand. Erase any unnecessary lines.

44

4. Add tiny semicircles with guidelines radiating out from them to the bottom edge of the wings. Draw a triangular shape at each outside edge of the wing corners. Halfway into each wing, draw a curved line. Add eyes and a beak to the head. Begin adding the clothing with wrist and ankle bands. The shirt and pants hang loose at their bands. Draw folds at the elbows and bottom of the chest. Also add folds to the back of the knee that is visible. Erase any unnecessary lines.

5. Complete the structure of the wings. Use the wing guidelines to segment individual plastic feather sections from the inner curved lines to the outside edges. Add a collar to the shirt. Draw the shoulder straps with a pouch hanging from them. Add some extra detail to the folds in the clothing. Place nostrils on the beak. Erase any unnecessary lines.

6. Add tone and shading. Give the wings a very smooth texture. Darken the eyes and add highlights. Add detail to the collar, straps, and pouch. Shade the wrist and ankle bands to look like metal. Your bird-man is ready to soar.

Life on this alien's world evolved differently from life on Earth. The crystalline form of these aliens is due to the extreme gravity and high temperatures of their planet. They have become the greatest miners of minerals and jewels in the galaxy.

1. Begin this sturdy fellow with a triangular head shape overlapping a larger triangle for his body. (Remember to avoid round shapes in this creature.)

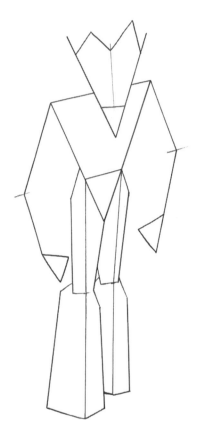

2. Cut an *M* shape into the top triangle. Erase the unneeded lines. Draw guidelines for the arms and elbows. Add triangular shapes at the ends of the guidelines for hands. Draw a line down the center of the head, then another across the small triangle, near the bottom, for the eyes. Sketch another line across the large triangle for his waist. Create guidelines to begin the legs. Add large solid shapes to further form the upper and lower legs.

3. Now add geometric shapes to form arms. Give him some thickness by adding sides to the head and body. Think of these shapes as boxes. Begin to add detail to the face by adding the eyes, eyebrows, nose, and cheekbones.

4. As you add the upper chest area, think of it as a thick piece of cardboard lying on his shoulders. Break up some of the shapes in the arms, hands, and legs with extra lines to detail the crystal body. Further define his facial features. Erase any unnecessary lines.

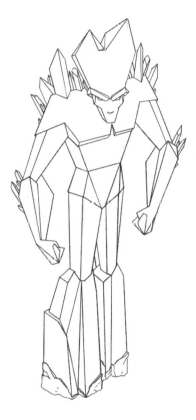

5. With the basic outline completed, now add detail. To make your creature look more sinister, add multiple pyramid and box shapes to his shoulders and arms. Draw as many or as few of these shapes as you like. Connect any loose lines together as triangles to form facets, much like those in diamonds and other jewels. At the bottom of his feet, you can add some rough, rocky shapes to give him an unpolished texture, as if he has done a lot of walking.

6. Finally, add dark shading to one side of the creature. Fill in his feet. After you add lighter shading and highlight lines to the front surfaces, your crystalline alien is complete.

47

A starship commander not only has to have great tactical skills in times of conflict but also diplomatic expertise when dealing with cultures from other planets. Starship commanders who have risen to the top are given command of galactic cruisers.

1. Begin with an oval shape for the head. Draw her torso and add a center line. Sketch guidelines for the arms and legs with lines for the elbows and knees. Add basic shapes for her hands and feet.

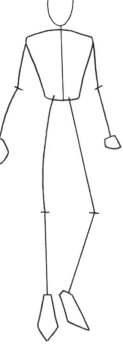

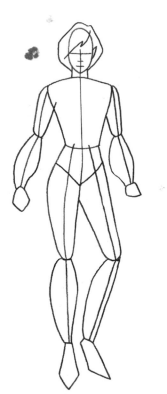

2. Draw guidelines for her facial features and the one ear that shows. Now add hair. Sketch the basic shape of the pelvic area. Fill in the outline of her neck, arms, and legs.

3. Now start adding detail to her uniform. Draw shoulder pads and knee guards. Finish the neck by adding a semicircle just slightly wider than the neck itself. Add thick padding around each elbow and solid bands around the wrists. Detail each of her hands. Her right hand is human, but her left hand has biomechanic enhancements with very angular metal fingers. Make the bottoms of her legs flair out a little with triangular shapes. These will be the lower parts of her leg guards. Put soles on the bottoms of her shoes.

4. Add details to her face and hair. Give her almond-shaped eyes, eyebrows, and indicate her nose and mouth. Start giving the uniform some shape and creases. Build the collar with a *V* shape in the center just under the chin. Add a belt with a holster hanging from it. Be sure to include a blaster in the holster. Shape the leg guards to be wider at the top and bottom. Give her left hand some more mechanical detail. Erase any unnecessary lines.

5. Finalize the details of her body and uniform. Little things help give realism to your starship commander, such as fine lines in her hair, details in the hardware of the uniform, and creases in the cloth. Erase any unnecessary lines.

6. When shading, make the cloth of the uniform a little darker than the rest of the uniform. Place the light source over her head and to her right. Draw some horizontal lines to detail the knee area of her leg guards. When you work on her face, shade one side of the nose all the way up to her left eyebrow. Make the upper line on her mouth darker and thicker than the bottom line. This will give her fuller lips. Finally, go in and find the areas you want to make black, like the belt and other places that need the heaviest shading.

This mighty robot is remote controlled by a person wired into a virtual suit. Every action that the person does is transmitted and duplicated by the robot. These robots can be sent into battle from a location far away when conditions are not suited for people.

1. Begin by drawing a square and a triangle. This is the side of the robot's torso area.

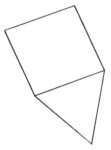

2. Add the front to the torso. Across the top of the torso, draw a line with a circle at each end. This is the shoulder section. Draw a line parallel to the shoulder line through the center of the triangle.

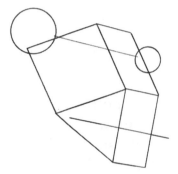

3. From each of the shoulder circles, draw guidelines for the arms with lines at the elbows. Add hand shapes. Sketch the leg guidelines a little way out from the torso. Draw lines at the knees and a baseline for the legs.

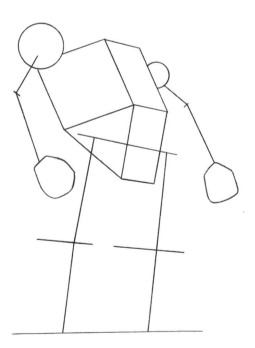

4. Create a large box for each of the forearms. The upper arms are smaller boxes that fit into the larger ones and connect to the shoulders. Add another box to each of the upper legs. Erase any unnecessary lines.

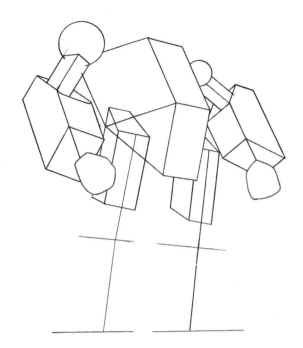

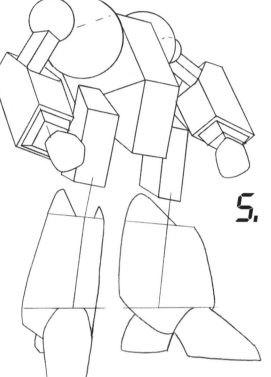

5. Draw large circles between the shoulders and torso. Now add the wrist area with a box between the forearm and hand on each arm. Using the leg guidelines, sketch the lower leg units as somewhat oblong shapes that will cover the lower moving parts. Below these, add the front and heel shapes to the feet. Erase any unnecessary lines.

6. Add another box inside each forearm box to connect them to the upper arms. Add another circle within the large circle of the near shoulder housing only. The knees are now drawn as boxes that connect to the back of the legs with small disks. The ankles are also disk shapes but much larger. Set them into the lower leg units by cutting into the units around the disks. This is similar to the way tires are set into a twentieth-century car's fenders. Erase any unnecessary lines.

7. Add the domed head unit to the top of the torso. Split the near shoulder housing with a curved line. Begin the hose that connects the housing to the shoulder. Break the hand shapes into thumbs and fingers. Connect the near upper leg to the torso with a mostly hidden oval. Add definition to the lower leg units with lines that separate the fronts and the sides. Do the same with the feet by adding lines to make them three-dimensional.

8. Finish your battle-bot by adding more tubes under the shoulder, then breaking the fingers and thumbs into smaller segments. Add tone and shading to your battle-bot to make it look smooth. Give the glass visor white streaks. Your battle-bot is now ready for battle.

The Frozen Tundra Transport, or FTT, is the best form of transportation on ice-covered planets. Its twin pulse engines propel it forward while the three navigational blades slice across the slick surface with great maneuverability. The FTT can seat six people with room for the family penguin.

1. The FTT starts with a simple six-sided shape that is cut in half with a vertical line down the middle. Draw guidelines from each point that will have a visible side.

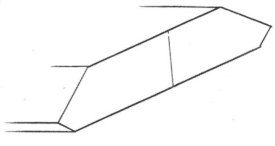

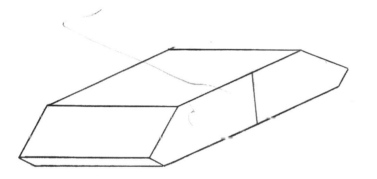

2. Extend these guidelines and add a far side to create a box shape.

3. Draw a small rectangular box on the front of the FTT. Add both of the side lifters. The near lifter will be more visible than the other one.

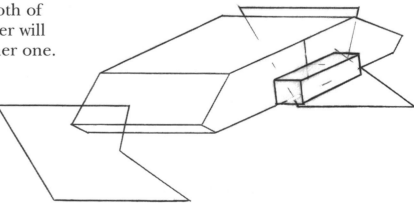

4. Add rectangles to the bottom of the side lifters. These are navigational blades. Create a ridge that runs over the top of the FTT. Sketch a guideline that extends forward from the center line on the front of the vehicle. Erase any unnecessary lines.

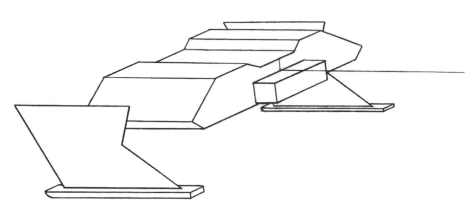

5. Using the guideline you just made, draw the nose unit of the FTT. Think of it as a tube that sticks into the front of the main box. The lower half of the tube sits inside the rectangular box on the front of the FTT. Add a curved, triangular shaft to the front of the tube and place an oval inside. Draw thin lines on the sides of the lifters to create a three-dimensional look.

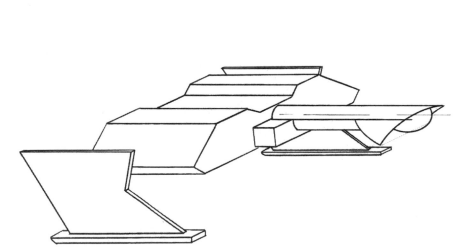

6. Draw the dome on top of the transport and extend it past the back end of the main shape. Add the curved base for the back of the dome to sit in. Place two long tubes under the transport for the pulse engines.

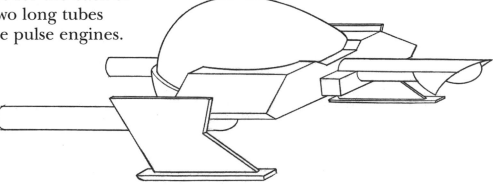

7. Add detail to the pulse engines at both ends. Under the front tube, draw the long navigational blade.

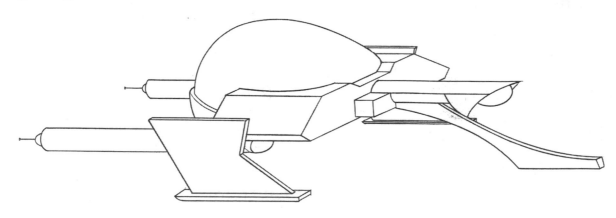

8. Finally, add shading and tone to the FTT. Make the dome look smooth and glassy by erasing a white oval in the center of it that gradually gets darker as you move away from the center. Add a symbol on the side, just below the dome. Your FTT is all set to race across any frozen wasteland.

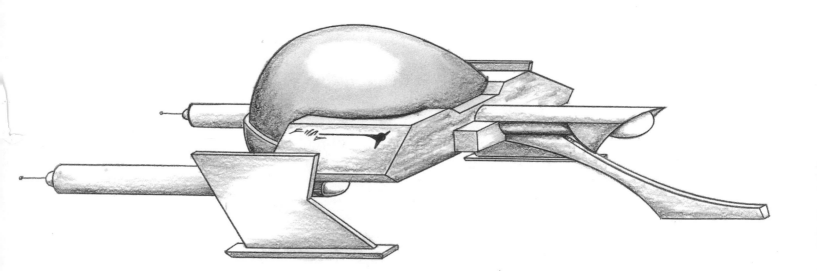

The Venusian Princess rules over a planet that hides under dense clouds. Not much is known about the secretive Venusians, since they rarely leave their planet or allow outsiders to land on the surface. Some outstanding features of the Venusians are their tattooed faces and silver eyes.

1. Draw an oval for the princess's head. Sketch guidelines for the facial details. Draw the torso with a center line that is off to one side. Add the guidelines for her arms with lines at the elbows. Put in the shapes for the hands. Instead of drawing guidelines for legs, just extend the center line down to where her feet would be. Sketch a line at the bottom of this line and another halfway up, where her knees would be.

2. Draw the princess's dress from the waist to feet level. Curve both sides out from the waist and come back in at the knees. The knee area will be as thick as the waist. At the bottom of the dress, sketch small lines to indicate where the feet will go. Add triangular shoulder flares out over the arms. Finish the shape of her neck, then draw the collar of her cape. The top of the collar is a downward curving line. Draw another line above the eye line and extend the center line above her head. This will be her crown. Add detail to her right hand.

Drawing Tip: Using the basic form of this princess, you can create other female characters by drawing different clothes and head features.

3. Complete the shape of the crown with three prongs on top and sides that go down to her chin. Add hair to the back of her head and down the back of her neck, held in place by a small cylinder. Draw her eyes, nose, and mouth using the guidelines. Finish the collar with two small triangles attached to her dress. Give the princess wide sleeves with cuffs that are tight on the wrist. Place her belt around her waist. Draw a long cape that curves around at the bottom. Using the guides for the feet, give her pointed shoes. Make a fold in the right side of the dress at the knees. Erase any unnecessary lines.

4. Place an oval-shaped jewel in the center of her crown. Draw tattoos on the princess's forehead and around her eyes. Add a collar around her neck and draw some more jewels beneath it. Fill in more details on the sleeves, dress, and belt.

5. Complete your princess by adding tone and shading. Small pencil specks around the cape give it a richer cloth texture.

Android servants are very useful around the house. They can clean, garden, and repair things, as well as cook gourmet meals. They have access to vast resources of knowledge, enabling them to assist their masters in any subject.

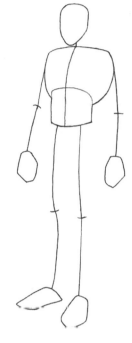

1. Start the android with an oval head that is slightly flat on the sides. Sketch the torso. Unlike the other basic torsos in this book, this one will be broken into two parts to include the chest. Add the center line and connect the head to the torso with a neckline. Draw guidelines for the arms and legs with lines for the elbows and knees. Sketch shapes for the hands and feet.

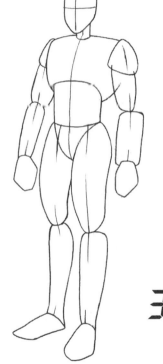

2. Draw a center line on the head and a line for the eye placement. Add shoulder units and a triangular pelvic area. Continue the center line through the pelvic area. Fill in the shapes for the arms, legs, and neck.

3. Now go back up to the head and add a rectangular eye unit, a circle for the mouth, and earpieces. Draw a base around the neck. Place hinged joints in the elbows. Sketch an arm guard on the android's right forearm. Add a torso shield from the lower line of the chest to slightly below the pelvic area. Define the hands. At the knees and ankles, add joint shields. Erase any unnecessary lines.

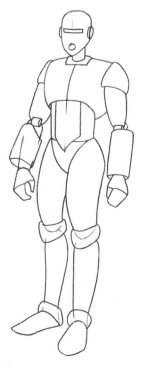

4. Further detail your android by adding antennae to the ears and speaker lines to the mouth. Define the jawline and back of the head and add dots that screw the face together. Break the neck into smaller segments. Finish the structure of the arms by adding wires, screws, and a cylindrical unit to the right arm. Break the hands into more segments and bolt them together between the thumb and fingers. Segment the feet and bolt them together as well. Add an open hip socket to the android's left leg. Erase any unnecessary lines.

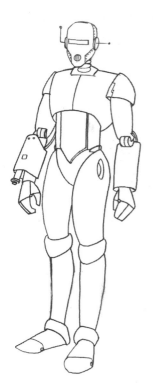

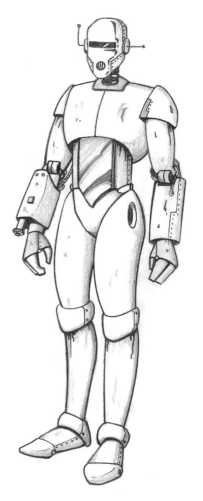

5. Shade your android to look like it is made out of plastic and metal. Put a white highlight in the eye unit to give it a glassy look. Highlight the torso shield. Add more detail to the body with lines that have screws running along them. At the knee and shoulder joints, draw oil drips to make the android look older. Place some dirt and dings on the android as well and it is ready to serve.

On a very remote planet in the Synora System, there is a group of mystics that has rejected science and turned to magic. Legend says that these mystics are over a thousand years old.

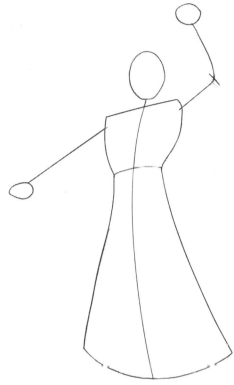

1. Start by drawing an oval shape for the head. At the base of the head, draw a center line down the figure. Just below the head, draw a shoulder line that is angled up on the left side of the figure. Add a curved line to indicate the waist. Connect the shoulders to the waist on both sides. This will be the chest area. From the waist, continue these lines by curving them out and down almost as far as the center line. Finish the shape of the inner cloak by joining the two sides together at the bottom with a curved line. Add guidelines for the arms with two round shapes at the ends for hands. Bend the mystic's left arm at the elbow and put a line there.

2. Now draw the basic shape of the outer cloak. The hood should fit loosely over the head and widen on the shoulders. Make the sleeves very big and loose as well. The left sleeve should only extend out from the shoulder to the cross line at the elbow. The main part of the cloak should extend from the hood down the length of the figure. Be sure to billow the cloak away from the body to give your character some action. Add a center line to the face and guidelines for the eyes, nose, and mouth.

3. Add more detail to the cloak by drawing lines to indicate folds in the fabric. Finish the bottom of the cloak. Draw the sash at the waist with two lines that end at a small circle on the side. Begin adding some detail to the face and neck. When you have the shape of the neck defined, sketch a collar for the inner cloak. Break the small round shapes of the hands into fingers and thumbs. Add a line that extends out from both sides of the left hand. This will be the energy staff. Halfway between the hand and elbow of the left arm, add a small oval. This will be the opening of the shirtsleeve.

4. Complete the sleeve and draw the left forearm. Draw the energy staff with three prongs at one end. Taper it so that it is smaller at the back end. Give your mystic large eyes and a small half-circle nose. At the waist, break up the small circle to look like a tied knot and add two long pieces of cloth to finish the sash. Now draw the large tail. Erase any unnecessary lines.

5. Detail the tail by adding some scales. These will be much less visible in the finished drawing. Finish the face by adding bags under the eyes and detail to the nose and mouth. Fit a circle into the three prongs of the energy staff. Complete the clothing with a few more lines to indicate folds. Erase any unnecessary lines.

6. Finish your mystic with detail on the wood of the staff and a glow from the globe. Use this glow as your light source and make anything that faces it lighter than the rest of your figure. Shade the inner portions of the drawing. Give the cloak some texture and dirt specks. Make the scales look much lighter by giving them a smudged effect. Finally, add a shadow to the ground under the ancient mystic.

Basically, perspective is used to make objects in your drawing look solid or three-dimensional. Using a ruler, you will take a simple shape like a square and turn it into a box with sides.

THE HORIZON LINE

The first thing you need to do is find the horizon line in your drawing. The horizon line is your eye level.

In this first example, the eye level, or horizon line, is above the object being drawn. This will give you the feeling of looking down at the object. First, lightly draw the horizon line. Now draw the front, or the closest plane of the box, where you want it to be. Next, pick a point on the horizon line that is referred to as the vanishing point. Connect the points of the box to this vanishing point. Finally, add the back of the box by keeping the lines on each side parallel to each other.

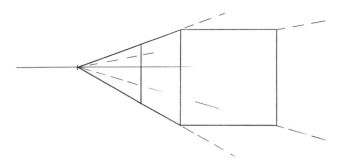

Now try the same thing with the box, but change the horizon line so you are at the same level as the box.

Try this again, but move the horizon line low in the drawing so the box will now appear to be overhead.

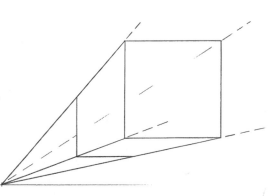

This example is just a simple box, but it can be applied to any object. You will find that if you place objects inside of boxes, you will be able to figure out how they look in perspective.

63

You've drawn cyborgs, soldiers, androids, and all sorts of vehicles, but don't let your sci-fi journey end just yet! The best aliens and space transporters are still to be drawn, for those are the pictures that you create in your mind.

Take the drawing tips and suggestions that you've learned throughout this book and start developing your very own futuristic universe. You may want to use the basic foundations of some of the drawings shown here and use your imagination to alter them in your own distinctive style.

Explore what a city would look like in your future galaxy. How would a school be structured? A playground? You can even create your own personal android servant, custom designed to fit your specific desires.

Most of all, have fun, and keep your pencils sharp and your eyes on the stars!